Discovering

Ohio

Discovering

Ohio

Text: Barbara J. Shangle
Concept and Design: Robert D. Shangle

First Printing February, 2001
American Products Publishing Company
Division of American Products Corporation
6750 SW 111th Avenue, Beaverton, Oregon 97008

"Learn about America in a beautiful way."

Library of Congress Cataloging-in-Publication Data

Shangle, Barbara -
    Discovering Ohio / text, Barbara Shangle.
        p. cm.
    ISBN 1-884958-64-8 (hardcover) – ISBN 1-884958-63-X (pbk)

    1. Ohio—Pictorial works. 2. Ohio—Description and travel. 3. Ohio—   History. I. Title

    F492.S5 2001
    977.1—dc21   00-067516

Copyright © 2000 by Robert D. Shangle
Printed in Hong Kong by Palace Press
Concept, Publishing and Distribution by
American Products Publishing Company
Beaverton, Oregon USA

Contents

Introduction

When inquiring men came into the area that is now Ohio, they found, quite simply, the largest deciduous hardwood forest in the world. Under the trees was land that could double or triple the yield of the thin New England soil. Under the land surface, though no one knew it at first, were other riches that would effect the value of the area: oil, natural gas, coal, and iron ore. It was the sort of place where success seemed assured, and all that was needed was someone to do the work.

Emigrants were not long in coming. When Ohio joined the Union on March 1, 1803, as the seventeenth state, 196 years had passed since the first permanent settlement on American shores had occurred. The eastern seaboard was crowded, society stratified, and *opportunity* was in short supply. Settlers started trickling into Ohio, struggling through the Appalachian Mountains and moving down the Ohio River in flatboats. Wherever the boats were landed, the settlers made clearings and planted crops, thinned the dark forests that permitted sunlight to permeate the fertile ground for the first time.

The new land seemed to produce a new attitude; even very early, observers made note of the buoyant optimism that permeated Ohio, the yeasty mix of people and resources that made things happen fast. Perhaps it was the fresh start where, lacking a common past, people invested together in the future. Certainly the natural richness of the land encouraged optimism and accomplishment. It was a place in those early years, at least, where a man's abilities were his only limitations, and where hard work *would* pay off. The earth offered of itself in ways the settlers had never dreamed of, and progress seemed inevitable.

The people of Ohio found out soon enough that there is such a thing as *too much progress*, and being keen of mind they came up with a solution. Call it progressivism: the ability of a people to evaluate what they are doing; to build on accomplishments; to master progress and to make it work for them. Agriculture is an example of progressivism. Progress produced so much wheat in the new frontier that it was burnt for fuel or used to fill mud holes. So, progressive people built canals to get the crop to market. When it became apparent that the world would buy all of the grain Ohio could produce, progressive farmers developed the nation's first mechanical reaper to help them keep up with the demand. And when their lands started to wear out from overuse, progressive Ohio farmers began research on land conservation and crop diversification. Every move has been one of gain.

Progressivism was not restricted only to agriculture; but improved thinking created diversification, producing the first fruits of success in other ways. Runaway industrialization produced exploitation and corruption, while at the same time, progressivism produced the nation's first unemployment compensation program and the author of the Sherman Anti-Trust Act. Progress produced environmental pollution, overgrazing, over logging, and runaway erosion. Educated Ohioans, seeing what they had wrought, developed the nation's first nature conservancy.

Ohioans know that in spite of the soap, pottery, matches, Bibles, rubber products, playing cards, golf balls, pumps, power shovels, cash registers, and coffins, in whose production they are a world leader, everything still comes back to the land. Farming is still one of the largest single industries in Ohio.

Outside of the major metropolitan areas, the Ohio countryside continues to offer up its riches. The list of Ohio's agricultural products reads like a menu: livestock, poultry and eggs, wheat, sugar beets, maple syrup, rye, vegetables, orchard fruits, gallons and gallons of wine per year, and tobacco. Industrial Ohio attracts most of the attention, but the traveler who gets outside of town will find a country that still treasures and depends on the good land that was there in the first place.

The pioneering settler changed Ohio's face more than anything else since the Ice Age. Only a fleeting glimpse remains of the great hardwood forest. It was cleared, stump by painful stump, so that Ohioans could grow food, transport it to market, fuel the steel mills, pump the oil, make the glass, and supply industry with its raw materials. The land has been used and, in some cases, it has almost been depleted.

However, man's influence on the land has not been all bad, and Ohio, early to reap the consequences of irresponsibility, has made haste to improve its stewardship. As a result of the responsible action, a traveler in Ohio will see rich and well-managed croplands, groves of sugar maples, lush pastures; while lands that never should have been plowed are being reforested. Then there are the lakes. In the early days of Ohio's existence, there were about 6,700 acres of natural lakes, while today about 100,000 acres is under water. Reservoirs were built to feed the canals, and later reservoirs were built to impound water for navigation or for relief from the disastrous flooding that has plagued Ohio for all of its history. The lakes attract migratory waterfowl, wildlife, and people.

Mindful of their ties to the land and to their need for natural beauty, Ohioans have been far from backward in reserving for public use the beautiful, the primitive, and the unusual land within their state boundaries. Parks dot the Lake Erie shoreline and the Hocking Valley, underlain by sandstone that was once the shoreline of an earlier lake. It shows in its fascinating erosion patterns just what a river can do when a glacier hurries it along.

In other places Ohio has memorialized its history, the remnants of the

the Ohio and Erie Canal in Miami County, and its prehistory in the Indian burial mounds that appear throughout the state. Even the conservation movement, itself, has been honored. Ohio Power Company Recreation Area in northeastern Morgan County is a rehabilitated strip mine where clear running streams and narrow, winding valley lakes have brought even the beaver back to land once mined for coal to produce electricity. The Malabar Farm, once the home and laboratory of conservationist farmer and author Louis Bromfield, is now a state park and a monument to the conservation movement.

Typically for Ohio, preserving the land has turned out to be good business. Ohio was not the first state to awaken from 19th-century capitalism to find itself polluted, eroded, and overgrazed, but it *was* the first state to develop a nature conservancy district. The $40-million expense of the first project has already had direct benefits of more than $90-million, and Ohio's example has served as a model for federal legislation. Another success story is the reforestation and regeneration of energy, education, and ingenuity brought forth by the people of Ohio. That illustrates the real contribution to progress that has always been part of the Ohio character.

Ohio will never again be covered by the world's greatest deciduous hardwood forest. That distinction is gone with the Native Americans who once walked the forest trails and camped in the great subterranean caves. This land, once a playground for the massive forces of ice-aged glaciers, is now gently rolling farmland, reshaped by man. But because of man wanting to improve what is around him, Ohio is still beautiful, more beautiful perhaps because it is more appreciated by those people who, in a day of industrialization, still know the value of their land.

The problem with a book like this is selection. How can a small book deal with such a big subject? The four dozen photographs presented can only suggest the beauty of the free and wild spaces of Ohio, the orderly farms, the mighty rivers, the canyons, lakes, and waterfalls. It is only a hint of what *is* Ohio, and then perhaps just enough to whet the appetite and flatter the pride of those Ohioans and others who want to know what lies outside the greater metropolitan areas that get most of the attention. *Discovering Ohio* is offered as an appetizer. The reader is responsible for discovering the main course, the state of Ohio, on his own.

The Preamble
To the Constitution

We, the people of the State of Ohio,
grateful to Almighty God
for our freedom,
to secure its blessings
and promote our common welfare,
do establish this Constitution.

Entered the Union as the
Seventeenth state on March 1, 1803

State Motto:

"With God All Things Are Possible"

Adopted in 1958.
The first motto adopted by the state
was abandoned after a few years.
The current motto was adopted at the
urging of a 12-year-old boy from Cincinnati.

Southern Ohio

The Ohio River flows from the coal hills of eastern Ohio to the cornbelt area of the southwestern section of the state, defining the south border of Ohio. Early settlers struggled through the Appalachian Mountains to Pittsburgh, navigating the Ohio River on flatboats until they found some place to put ashore. In the absence of other highways, the "shining road" of the Ohio River, broken only once along its length by rapids, provided a main means of transportation into a new frontier. Centuries later, it is still an important shipping artery, though no longer the only one available.

If you were to put a flatboat into the river at Pittsburgh, Pennsylvania, today, in order to duplicate the journey made in the 1780s and '90s by Ohio's settlers, the first half of the journey would be made through fairly industrialized and developed country. (The Ohio River is formed by the confluence of the Allegheny and Monongahela rivers at Pittsburgh). The shipping of iron ore and coal, and the production of steel and ceramic products kept the river bustling with traffic; the river banks were developed to receive and discharge the freight that was carried up and down the river.

Below Portsmouth, however, in the southern extremity of the state, the landscape changes to a serene, pastoral setting. In some areas fields and forests roll down almost to the water's edge, smaller creeks and rivers intersect, and it is possible, discounting a few locks and dams, to get an idea of how things looked in an earlier time. The peaceful river flows at about three-miles-per-hour, regulated now by dams and canals to provide the constant depth needed for year-round navigation. Where the river bends gracefully to disappear between wooded hills, perhaps the 285-foot *Delta Queen,* the grand and elegant 19th-century-era sternwheeler, which still plies the Ohio River waters, will make a stately appearance through the sunlit haze. Just for an instant the river offers its immutable experience: time might be suspended, and you may murmur, ". . . so *this* is how is was." It seems to be the nature of rivers everywhere to allow people, occasionally, to become released in time, and the Ohio River will show you where it has been if you are patient.

The river was there before the settlers arrived, and so were the Indian Mounds that make their presence in southwestern Ohio. It is another kind of experience in timelessness to ponder the massive earthworks of these forgotten peoples. Tremper Mound, outside of Portsmouth, several sites in Ross County around the city of Chillicothe, and three sites on U.S. Highway 50 and Ohio Highway 41 between Chillicothe and West Union have been set aside as memorials to these people. In other places within the state, the farmers plow, road construction equipment, and archaeological probing have unearthed bones, tools, and weapons of the vanished mound builders. It has been possible to recognize these distinct cultures from the artifacts they left behind.

Later and more primitive cultures such as Adena and Fort Ancient sometimes overlap the Hopewell remains. Fort Ancient, which was a Hopewell ceremonial site some 2,000 years ago, was later occupied by the Fort Ancient culture, which is characterized by crude pottery, ornaments of stone, bone, and shell, and generally non-cremated human remains. Today, a nature trail offers picturesque views of the Miami River Valley on the way to the three "forts" at the Fort Ancient site. The Adena culture, more advanced than Fort Ancient but less-so than the Hopewell who preceded them, were responsible for the great conical mounds that contained single or multiple burials as well as copper, fabric, and beaded artifacts.

The largest, most spectacular and famous of the prehistoric Indian earthworks is the Serpent Mound, located on State Highway 73 between Loudon and Locust Grove. The mound is in the shape of a wriggling snake with an egg in its jaws. Built by the Adena Indians for some unknown ceremonial purpose, the mound unwinds for 1,300 feet across a gentle hilltop through a grove of trees. An observation platform allows a panoramic view that provides a chance to absorb the historical mystery of this strange place.

A few other locations near the Ohio River give you a chance to think back to days gone by—way back. North of Chillicothe is the Mound City Group National Monument, a large geometric complex known as the "City of the Dead." Twenty-three mounds surrounded by an earth enclosure served some ceremonial function at about the time of Christ. And in northern Jackson County near the village of Leo, northwest of Jackson on U.S. Highway 35, is the Leo Petroglyph. This large rock outcrop provided an opportunity for some ancient prehistoric artist or artists, probably Fort Ancient Indians, to leave a mark for future investigation. Many objects are recognizable: birds, fish, a mammal that is most likely a bear, human feet, and animal tracks. The messages, if in fact they are messages and not just prehistoric doodling, have so far escaped translation.

History along this part of the Ohio stretches back so far that it is completely out of mind sight: before the white man's presence, there were the Native Americans; before the Native Americans there were *others*, earlier Native Americans—and before that, there were glaciers. Southwestern Ohio owes much of the variety of its landscape to the effects of the tons of ice that once ended there. Even the lands that were not scoured by the massive ice caps were eroded by the runoff when they melted. Some of the streams that were blocked by ice and rubble were forced to relocate through higher ground. Generally, the result is rolling landscape, punctuated in places by a deep gorge that was cut through bedrock as the glacial melt added power to the displaced streams.

Some of the deep gorges created by the moving glaciers are spectacular enough so that some have been preserved as state parks, although many remain private property. Caesar Creek, Seven Caves, and Rocky Fork are samples that belong to the public. Caesar Creek and Rocky Fork are on lake reservoirs of the same names, and Seven Caves is only a short distance from Rocky Fork.

Caesar Creek is a few miles east of Waynesville on State Highway 73, between Interstate Highway 71 on the south and U.S. Highway 42 on the west in southwest Ohio. The deep valley of Caesar Creek Gorge was carved out by great quantities of glacial meltwater. The canyon walls rise a breathtaking 180 feet above the valley floor, and the exposed limestone is rich in fossils. On the eastside of the lake is Caesar Creek State Park.

Similar forces created the Rocky Fork Valley, east of Hillsboro off of U.S. Highway 50 in southern Ohio. The gentle topography is due to glacial smoothing and deposits that filled the original stream valley. In the lower valley, below the dam that impounds Rocky Fork Lake, it is possible to see the seventy-five-foot gorge-cut created by the Wisconsonian glacier. On the south side of the lake is Rocky Fork State Park.

The Seven Caves, likewise created by the erosive power of glacial meltwater, are found about fifty feet above Rocky Fork Creek. Trails have been developed to give hikers access to the caves. This area, with deep rugged gorges, winding streams with waterfalls, and lush vegetation among the rocks and in the valleys, inspire a sense of wonder. The caves are rich in Shawnee Indian lore.

Just northeast is Paint Creek State Park, equipped with a reservoir lake created by the damming of Paint Creek. Nearby is impressive Paint Creek Pioneer Farm, a living museum equipped with a vintage log house, log barn and livestock, other log buildings, plus a maintained garden and crop fields.

Farther north and west on U.S. Highway 27, right up against the Indiana State border, is another area worth visiting for a feel of the "original" Ohio: Hueston Woods State Park, outside of College Corner. Though surrounded by products of human engineering, Hueston Woods presents a 200-acre forest

Marblehead Lighthouse, Marblehead Peninsula, Lake Erie

This sixty-five foot structure, the oldest active lighthouse on the Great Lakes, was built in 1821 and has acted as a navigational guide since 1822 along the shore of Lake Erie and to the entrance of Sandusky Bay. This structure will never be blown over by the massive gale winds that can speed over the waters of the lake, as the twenty-five foot base has walls five feet thick, thinning to a mere two feet thick at the twelve-foot-height level. The initial light works began as whale oil lamps, replaced by kerosene lamps in 1858. Electricity was introduced in 1923, increasing the candlepower of the light and making the maintenance much easier. The light was automated in 1958. Civilian lighthouse keepers were replaced by the United State Coast Guard in 1946. Though the Coast Guard still maintains the lighthouse beacon, the Ohio Department of Natural Resources has maintained the property since 1972 and took ownership of the light tower in 1998. Lighthouse tours are quite popular, but seasonal.

Photography by Shangle Photographics

Ohio State Capitol in the city of Columbus

Though not the first choice as the site for Ohio's capital, Columbus received the nod following the donation of ten acres of land on the east side of the Scioto River by some Franklinton citizens. Government offices were moved from Chillicothe to Columbus in 1816. The Greek Revival, Doric colonnade building was begun in 1839, built of Ohio limestone quarried from the Scioto River. The highly regarded center rotunda emulates the design of the Greek Parthenon. The original design failed to provide a heating and ventilation system, but the problem was solved by one of the seven architects that were overseers of the construction. Problems plagued the architects and contractors, but eventually the building was completed in 1861.

Photography by Robert D. Shangle

Upper Falls at Old Man's Cave, Hocking Hills State Parks, Southeast Ohio

Old Man's Cave, one of three recessed caves found in the Hocking Hills State Park in Hocking County — Ash Cave and Cantwell Cliffs are the other two — is a delightful location found within the sandstone hills. Created by eroding sandstone of various compositions over millions of years, the outcome has been most rewarding. Native Americans enjoyed the cool, moist environment complete with deep gorges, naming the area *Hockhocking* for the bottle-shaped Hocking River. The state purchased the first 146 acres in 1924, which included the Old Man's Cave, long aware of its scenic beauty since 1870. Three additional areas have been added, Rock House, Conkles Hollow and Cedar Falls, creating a total of six parks. The state provides excellent amenities: miles of hiking trails, picnic shelters, lodging facilities, extensive camping sites and a dining lodge.

Photography by Shangle Photographics

The Columbus Santa Maria in the city of Columbus, Scioto River, Central Ohio

Completed in 1992 to commemorate the 500th Anniversary of the discovery voyage by Christopher Columbus, the city of Columbus finds pride in the full-scale reproduction of the flag ship *Santa Maria*. The ship is moored at Battelle Park on the eastside of the Scioto River, very near the center of downtown Columbus. Tours are available aboard the vessel, displaying the fine detail of the ship and the intricate workings and area that would have provided home to its sailors. Columbus departed for the New World on August 3, 1492, and following a stay in the Canary Islands, he and his crew finalized the voyage across the Atlantic Ocean on October 12, 1492. At the time the Ohio legislature designated the area as the state's capital, it was determined that the city would be known as Columbus, honoring the great navigator.
Photography by Robert D. Shangle

Stan Hywet Hall, Home of F.A. Seiberling, co-founder of Goodyear Tire and Rubber Company, Akron

Tudor Revival architecture was the design of choice for the Seiberling family when the house was completed in 1915. Located on a seventy-acre estate that is complete with well-groomed formal gardens, the house is equipped with "21,000 panes of glass, 23 fireplaces, and hand-carved paneling of oak, sandalwood and black walnut [that] reflect the opulence of the era," so states Stan Hywet Hall. Original furnishings add authentic charm to the sixty-five room house.
Photography by James Blank

Lytle Park in downtown Cincinnati, Southwest Ohio

Cincinnati Parks states that Lytle Park is "An oasis of beauty in downtown Cincinnati's central business district, ...[and] features a panorama of floral displays changing from tulips, magnolia and crabapple in the spring to annuals and perennials in the summer and to annuals mixed with chrysanthemums in the fall . . . . The 2.31 acre park . . . is the original site of the Lytle family homestead, built in 1809 by General William Henry Lytle. Featured in the park is "an alle[y] of flags tracing the history of the Stars and Stripes; an ornamental wall with plaques depicting historic events which have occurred on this site; a monument dedicated to the U.S. Marine Corps; and the Michael Mullen bandstand used for free concerts for the public. . . . Park holdings constitute nearly 5,000 acres, which amounts to approximately 10% of Cincinnati's total land area."
Photography by James Blank

Ohio State University, Columbus, Central Ohio

Opening its doors as an academic center on September 17, 1873 to twenty-four students "at the old Neil farm just two miles north of Columbus. . . ," six male students were the first graduating class in 1878. Also in 1878 the official name of the institution of higher learning became The Ohio State University, leaving the original title, Ohio Agricultural and Mechanical College behind. The first woman student graduated in 1879. A member of the Big Ten Conference NCAA, "Ohio State [also] has the largest recreation and intramural program in the nation." The Ohio State University Marching Band is a favorite unit at any performing event, such as in the Ohio Stadium that accommodates 90,400 people.
Photography by James Blank

The Sternwheeler *Lorena* on the Muskingum River, Zanesville, Southeast Ohio

It is a leisurely and pleasant experience floating the Muskingum River aboard one of the country's favorite sternwheel boats, *Lorena,* moored at Zane's Landing, a short distance from downtown Zanesville. The memories of celebrities who have experienced *Lorena's* amenities add zest to the festive lore gathered within the boat. Dining cruises and just "let's have fun" cruises are a regular part of the river front activities at Zane's Landing. Canoeing is a special activity on the Muskingum River too, especially down river from Zanesville all the way south to Marietta on the Ohio River, about eighty miles in total and equal to an easy seven-day vacation trip. Camping facilities are available along the way and at the river locks. The overall length of the Muskingum is one-hundred-twelve-miles, beginning at Coshocton, some twenty miles north of Zanesville, at the confluence of the Walhonding and Tuscarawas rivers.
Photography by Robert D. Shangle

The Birthplace House of Thomas Alva Edison, Milan, North-Central Ohio

Born in the little house in Milan to parents Nancy and Samuel Edison on February 11, 1847, Thomas Alva Edison lived here to the age of seven, when his parents sold the house and moved to Port Huron. Forty-years later, in 1894, his sister, Marion Edison Page, purchased the house and in 1906 Edison became the owner to his birthplace home. As the inventor of the incandescent lightbulb, Edison is credited in bringing electricity to the homes of the nation. However, in 1923 Edison was shocked to learn that his little house was still without electric power. The house was opened as the Edison Birthplace Museum in 1947 depicting with close proximity the life-style present in the 19th century.

Photography by Shangle Photographics

Lawnfield, Home to James A. Garfield, 20th President of the United States, Mentor, east of Cleveland

The James A. Garfield National Historic Site had a meager beginning as a two-room structure built about 1832 that was expanded to a total of nine rooms in the 1850s. Garfield purchased the house in 1876 during the years of his successful government service to his country. "In early 1880 Garfield enlarged the house to a 20-room, three-story structure with a wide front porch." Having served nine terms as a U.S. Congressman and being elected to the U.S. Senate, Garfield was successful in election efforts as the nation's 20th President in 1881. An extensive museum displays books, papers, pictures, and memorabilia of Garfield and his family, and explains the untimely death by an assassin's bullet just 200 days into his presidency. Interpretive tours of the magnificent house are available under the direction of the National Park Service and Western Reserve Historical Society, viewing the nation's first Presidential Library and first-floor living quarters.

Photography by Robert D. Shangle

Rock and Roll Hall of Fame and Museum, Cincinnati

A spectacular building dedicated to a *spectacular* industry, music. The Rock and Roll Hall of Fame and Museum states it best when it says it "honors the legendary performers, producers, songwriters, disc jockeys and others who have made rock and roll the force in our culture that it is. . . . Once inducted [into the Hall of Fame], the artists are further honored when they are featured in the Museum's Hall of Fame exhibit, which includes a computerized 'juke box' containing virtually every song of every performer inductee; etched-glass signatures of the inductees; a film on three huge screens recounting their careers and music; and a display of artifacts from the current year's inductees."

Photography by James Blank

The city of Columbus, Central Ohio

From the western edge of the Scioto River, an easy view of the city of Columbus is a special attraction to those having a leisurely experience. Today Columbus is the largest city in Ohio, taking its roots back to the first settling days of 1797. Land was donated to the state in 1812 for the expressed purpose of establishing the state's capital in this centrally located area. Platting of the future city began and the name Columbus was bestowed upon the town, in honor of navigator Christopher Columbus. In 1834 Columbus incorporated as a city and in 1839 the new Capitol was begun, with completion in 1861. The city grew and spread, extending one-hundred-ninety-plus square miles. The greater metropolitan area now extends into a six-county region with Columbus as the core area. The historic German Village south of downtown is a classic example of the ethnic heritage and restoration efforts experienced in Columbus. The Ohio Historical Center, the Center of Science and Industry, the Columbus Zoo and Aquarium, the 1894 Franklin Park Conservancy, the numerous museums, art centers, city parks and playgrounds, the multiple colleges and universities located within the city and outlying areas all add to the importance of the people to the city's foundation of strength.

Photography by Robert D. Shangle

The Sherman House, Lancaster, Southern Ohio

This house is the birthplace to famous brothers, William Tecumsah Sherman, born February 8, 1820, a famous Civil War Union General, and John Sherman, born May 10, 1823, who was the author of the Sherman Antitrust Act and Secretary of the Treasury (1877-1881). General Sherman graduated from West Point in 1840; John became an accredited attorney in 1844. John served his country as a U.S. Congressman and Senator. William was a banker, educator, and military career officer achieving the rank of full general. He retired in 1883 after an illustrious career that saw colorful controversy in his Civil War achievements. William died February 14, 1891 in New York City, with his grave site in St. Louis, Missouri. John died October 11, 1900, with his grave site in Washington, D.C.

Photography by Robert D. Shangle

Wheatland Village at Hale Farm & Village, north of Akron, Northeast Ohio

Rich history of area life as found in the early 1800s is revealed in the homeland property of Jonathan Hale and his wife, who developed a home and farm on land he purchased in 1810. Some original buildings, many moved from outlying sites, have joined the original 1825 Hale House used to create the Western Reserve town of Wheatland, located nearby the farm, where period-dressed occupants greet you with open enjoyment. Discussions with "current town occupants" are presented in the "now time" of the 1848 Wheatland Township. The Western Reserve Historical Society received ownership of the land in 1956, following the death of the great-granddaughter of Jonathan Hale, Clare Belle Ritchie.

Photography by Robert D. Shangle

The city of Cincinnati on the Ohio River, Southwest Ohio

An eclectic architectural montage could well describe the interesting skyline of Cincinnati. The leisurely flow of the Ohio River, the southern state boundary at this point, separating the states of Ohio and Kentucky and the cities of Cincinnati and Covington, can stir memories of history and enthusiasm regarding surging flood waters, the old floating palaces, grain and coal barges, and emigrating settlers who floated the river toward a home and a fresh start in the *West*. Cincinnati maintains its original charm in historic, classical buildings, and projects the ability to meld the sleek, progressive lines of the new-image generation of architectural achievement. In 1975 the Roebling Suspension Bridge was listed on the National Register of Historic Places. This bridge was the first to span the Ohio River, formally dedicated in 1867. It is claimed that the Roebling Bridge was a prototype for the Brooklyn Bridge in New York City.
Photography by James Blank

Marietta College in the city of Marietta, Southeast Ohio

One of the most important items on the agenda for the new settlement was education. Marietta College was the answer, chartered in 1835. Honor goes to those who knew the importance of education and honor goes to those who gave their lives for freedom, as represented by the grand flags flying high above the campus. Receiving the first settlers in April of 1788 at the "east point of the fork between the Ohio and Muskingum [rivers]," the forty-eight hearty men set upon a task of civilizing what they planned to be their *home*. Order was guided for the town's design. The name of Marietta was chosen to honor France and the young queen, Marie Antoinette, for the assistance given to the struggling American country. A monument memorial, "Start Westward of the United States," has been erected in Marietta to honor those New England pioneers who trekked to the western frontier and established the first permanent settlement in the Northwest Territory under the landmark Ordinance of 1787.

Photography by Robert D. Shangle

Cantwell Cliffs, Hocking Hills State Parks, South-Central Ohio

Considered by many to be "the most picturesque in Hocking County," Cantwell Cliffs, located on the northern end of State Road 374, is considered more remote than the other five parks within the Hocking Hills group, but its beauty and mystification are well worth the effort needed to see the cliffs. The Park Service states that "The erosion caused by Buck Run accounts for the deep valley, steep cliffs and rock shelter under the cliff."

Photography by Shangle Photographic

The Harding Home, Marion, North-Central Ohio

Ohio provided Warren Harding the rich "growing up" experiences boys need. Warren G. Harding, the 29th President of the United States of America, was born in Blooming Grove, Ohio, on November 2, 1865. His youthful education took place in the public schools of Caledonia, while his college education was achieved at Ohio Central College. Moving to Marion in 1883, Mr. Harding worked at, then purchased, a newspaper. The following year, he and Florence Kling DeWolfe were married in the Harding Home they planned and built together. Prior to his U.S. Presidency, Warren Harding served his home state as State Senator and Lieutenant Governor; moving on to U.S. Politics as a U.S. Senator in 1914. Warren G. Harding was elected president in 1920 and served from 1921 to August 2, 1923, when he suddenly died from what was reported to be a cerebral hemorrhage. "The Harding Memorial Association restored the home to its turn-of-the-century appearance. The original gas lights, which had been wired for electricity, were restored; decorations were duplicated in detail; and original furnishings were returned to their former positions. The Press Building, built in 1920 for reporters working during the front-porch [Presidential] campaign, was transformed into a museum."
Photography by James Blank

The Holden Arboretum, Kirtland, Northeast Ohio

"Established in 1931 on 100 acres and accredited by the American Association of Museums, The Holden Arboretum is dedicated to collecting woody plants for ornamental and scientific merit for northeastern Ohio. Education, research, and conservation efforts juxtapose with the plant collections and natural areas to make The Holden Arboretum one of the nation's leading horticultural institutions," as stated by the Arboretum. Now expanded to over 3,400 acres of well defined and maintained landscape, Holden Arboretum has achieved the position as one of the largest of all arboretums in the United States. Designed to achieve the most in color for seasonal beauty, gardens enhance areas with such flowering plants as delicate lilacs, crabapples, spectacular rhododendrons with a rainbow of colors. The well-groomed Hedge Garden illustrates the varied achievements of hedge row plants; there are various conifers and nut trees. Color bursts forth, it appears, forever.

Photography by James Blank

The City of Cleveland and Lake Erie

It was 1796 and Moses Cleaveland arrived with a surveying party to scope the land in the new West. Gradually the area became populated, and records indicate that by 1802 there were seventy-six "free male inhabitants over the age of 21." Cleavland received status of county seat to the newly created Cuyahoga County in 1810 and was chartered "as a village" on December 23, 1814. (The spelling of Cleveland was changed in 1831, discontinuing the extra *a*.) Shipping on Lake Erie was in its early stages. The first steamship to serve Cleveland was *Walk-in-the-Water*. (Today, water transportation is a key element of the industrial economy of Ohio and Cleveland, as the steel industry "depends upon the movement of iron ore and limestone across the Great Lakes to Lake Erie ports.") (*Encyclopeadia Britannica* britannica.com) Cleveland began to develop into a more cosmopolitan city. Several newspapers began publications; multiple religious denominations had established churches; the canal era became ingrained; commercial enterprises were created providing the necessary amenities required to develop a thriving city. By 1840 Cleveland had a population exceeding 6,000 and Cuyahoga County exceeded 26,000 people. Viewing the success of the ingenuity and perseverance of the people of Cleveland and Cuyahoga County is easy to see, by the development and growth of the city. Planning and execution of those plans has created a city of pride and achievement.

Photography by James Blank

Brandywine Falls, Cuyahoga Valley National Recreation Area, Northeast Ohio

Brandywine Falls tumbles sixty-feet over layered rocks creating a dramatic wonderment. The waterfall is but one of many interesting places within the Recreation Area's 33,000 acres located between the cities of Cleveland and Akron.
Photography by Shangle Photographics

The *Becky Thatcher* on the Muskingum River, Marietta, Southeast Ohio

Vaudeville is alive and well in Marietta and if you listen closely, then *think about it*, the laughter and joy of audiences over the years will burst forth and you'll laugh too. That is what is important when you participate in the adventures on the *Becky Thatcher*. If that boat could talk, she would tell you of her adventurous days as the *Mississippi III*, working as an inspector boat for the Corps of Engineers; as a restaurant and museum in Hannibal, Missouri, when she got her new name and added to the melancholy memories of Samuel Clement's *Mark Twain*. In 1976 *Becky* moved to Marietta and became an authentic showboat. She is ready, today, to provide laughter and joy, for true family fun.

Photography by Robert D. Shangle

Shawnee State Park, west of Portsmouth, South-Central Ohio

As the largest of Ohio's State Parks, *extraordinary* is just one of many superlative words used to describe Shawnee State Park and the adjacent Shawnee State Forest — 60,000 acres located within the foothills of the Appalachian Mountains. The Department of Natural Resources states, "Once the hunting grounds of the Shawnee Indians, the region is one of the most picturesque in the state, featuring erosion-carved valleys and wooded hills. The rugged beauty of the area has earned it the nickname 'The Little Smokies.' ....Historians note that the Shawnee name means 'those who have silver,' as the tribe conducted considerable trade in this precious metal." Points of interest located within the Park are Tremper Mound, Serpent Mound, the Olde Wayside Inn, the 1810 House, and the Southern Ohio Museum and Cultural Center.

Photography provided by the Ohio Department of Natural Resources, Photographer Mike Williams

Slate Run Living Historical Farm, Columbus Metro Park, east of Ashville, Central Ohio

When you leave your car in the parking lot at Slate Run Living Historical Farm, you are really stepping away from today's fast pace and entering the 1880s. Planted fields frame the farmstead, and a small family garden shows vigilant care. Roaming chickens scratch their way about their large roaming pen, while others move in-and-out of their coop. The farm house reveals a true lived-in feeling, with parlor chairs and pretty knickknacks and colorful dishes displayed, revealing the pride of personal treasures. Oil lamps are ready and waiting for twilight with sparkling chimneys, ready to glow bright for the nighttime hours. The farm kitchen can surely be cozy on cold blustery days as the big wood stove sits center stage, ready for the cook to prepare bubbling stews and soups, and bake pies and cakes and crunchy bread. A typical farmhouse for a large family, with a steep stairway and bedrooms upstairs. Out through the back door to the fruit cellar and summer kitchen, or out to the side porch. A large red barn and implement buildings house the hay, farm equipment and protection for the animals. It is a delight to see the excitement on the faces of unexpecting children when they come face to face with a munching horse or cow. An investigative adventure is highlighted by the opportunity to self guide through a truly terrific experience.

Photography by Robert D. Shangle

Beaver Creek State Park and Pioneer Village, East-Central Ohio

Beaver Creek State Park is located within the forested woodlands of eastern Ohio a few miles north of East Liverpool and about thirty miles south of Youngstown, near the Ohio-Pennsylvania state border. Ohio State Parks state that "Beaver Creek State Park, in the foothills of the Appalachian Mountains, is one of Ohio's most scenic parks. The park includes Little Beaver Creek, a state and national wild and scenic river, and acres of forest wilderness. . . . Remnants of the Sandy and Beaver Canal, a spur off the Ohio-Erie Canal, are found throughout the park. . . . The Little Beaver Valley provided opportunity for water power and resulted in the construction of Gaston's Mill in 1837. The mill stands completely restored and today grinds whole wheat flour, corn meal and buckwheat flour on a seasonal basis. A pioneer village, adjacent to the mill, includes a log home, schoolhouse, blacksmith shop and a church." Little Beaver Creek is excellent for canoeing, providing a challenge to an experienced paddler. The State Parks reminds the boater to respect the water here and "use caution . . . as the river's immense power is often hidden." During the summer or winter, Beaver Creek State Park provides an excellent opportunity to experience some of the best scenery and natural playgrounds in Ohio.

Photography provided by Ohio Department of Natural Resources, Mike Williams, Photographer

Piqua Historic Area, north of Dayton in West-Central Ohio

This original house and farm, located on 174 acres and built by Colonel John Johnstone about 1815, includes several original out buildings. A section of the Miami-Erie Canal provides mule-drawn canal boat rides.

Photography by Shangle Photographics

Doyle Road Covered Bridge, Ashtabula County, Northeast Ohio

When in "Beautiful Ashtabula County" you know you are in Covered Bridge Country. The local citizens are particularly proud to boast that all sixteen bridges provide interesting history and most are functional and operational, spanning flowing streams and rivers. Since 1984 the annual Covered Bridge Festival has been held the second full weekend in October, and what an informative weekend it is. Not only is there information about each bridge, but local-color history about the surrounding communities, buildings, and activities that make Ashtabula County so inviting. Covered bridges date back to 1867 construction, most having experienced loving renovation. Some bridges are more "modern" having been built in the 1920s. And still capitalizing on the old romantic idea of passing through the covered bridge, the Ashtabula County Covered Bridge Festival headquartered in Jefferson states that there are plans for the construction of the longest and highest of all covered bridges in the United States, to span the Ashtabula River in Ashtabula/Plymouth townships, expected to be a length of 550 feet and a height of about 90 feet. The Doyle Road bridge shown here, once known as the Mullen Bridge, "is 94 feet long and spans Mill Creek. A carpenter from Vermont . . . built the bridge in 1868" and it experienced renovation in 1987. It is exceptionally attractive when decorated for the holiday season with twinkling lights and red velvet bows.

Photography provided by Ashtabula County Covered Bridge Festival, Jefferson, Ohio

A valley of farms in Holmes County, west of New Philadelphia near Berlin, North-Central Ohio

A patchwork of spring colors broadcast far and wide over Holmes County, near Berlin, often referred to as the Amish Heartland of Ohio. Located in north-central Ohio, this undulating land was once covered with dense hardwood forests. This pastoral setting reveals the beauty of the rolling countryside and productive farms. Records indicated that about "one-third of all Amish people [in the United States] reside in Ohio and there are significant Amish populations in at least 21 Ohio counties." It is stated that the Wayne/Holmes county area has the largest of the Amish communities. While traveling the country roads, it is important to be aware of the Amish Buggy. Efforts have been made between the Amish Community and the Ohio State University Extension for improvements for visual aids for the horse-drawn buggies while occupying the public highways for transportation needs.

Photography by James Blank

Paint Creek Pioneer Farm, east of Hillsboro in Highland County, Southwest Ohio

Paint Creek State Park is home to a unique Pioneer Farm nestled in the rolling hills of southern Ohio. The farm is equipped with a vintage log house, log barn and livestock. A well maintained garden and field display what is necessary for a self-sustaining farm in the early 1800s. Nearby is Paint Creek Reservoir, created by the damming of Paint Creek, once the source of power for processing mills. Camping, boating, hunting and fishing, swimming, picnicking, and hiking are great pastimes for vacationers who frequent the park. Wildflowers, birds and wildlife have always been abundant here.

Photography by Robert D. Shangle

Dunham Tavern Museum, 6709 Euclid Avenue, in the city of Cleveland

Listed in the Register of National Historic Places, the city of Cleveland has designated the Dunham Tavern as a Cleveland Landmark. This 1824 structure was built by Rufus and Jane Dunham, who came to the Western Reserve from Massachusetts in 1819. He was both a farmer and tavernkeeper, creating a center for political and social activities. Its history includes use as a private residence and artist studio. Saved by the Society of Collectors, who took over the management of the building as a museum, it has been open to the public since 1941.

Photography by Shangle Photographics

United States Airforce Museum, Wright-Patterson Airforce Base, Dayton

A feature attraction at Dayton is the United States Airforce Museum. Available aircraft on display date back as far as World War I. The museum is one of the oldest and largest military aviation museums in the world. Displays of military memorabilia include more than three-hundred aircraft, including advanced missiles and bombs used in Desert Storm and the Persian Gulf War. The Dayton Aviation Heritage National Historical Park pays honor to Paul L. Dunbar and Orville and Wilbur Wright.

Photography by Robert D. Shangle

The historic harbor district on Mosquito Creek, Ashtabula, Northeast Ohio

A pleasure craft just sounds its horn and the massive draw bridge makes a mighty lift, allowing the tall-masted sailboat to power on to its destination. The marina houses many pleasure craft that frequent waters of the area, which includes Lake Erie. Boating is a serious matter in the state of Ohio. Laws have been implemented requiring safety courses for boat operators. The Ohio Department of Natural Resources Division of Watercraft states that "No one under 12 years of age may operate a boat powered by more than 10 horsepower, personal watercraft excluded unless the person is under the direct visual and audible supervision, during the operation, of a person who is at least 18 years of age who is aboard the powercraft. A supervising person ... must hold a safe boater course or proficiency exam certificate."

Photography provided by the Ashtabula Convention and Visitors Association, Timothy Poe, Photographer

Malabar Farm, Lucas, southeast of Mansfield, North-Central Ohio

Outside the small town of Lucas, southeast of Mansfield in Richland County, is Malabar Farm, a monument to the beginning of the conservation movement in Ohio in the 1930s. Malabar, an Asian word meaning *beautiful valley*, was the home of native Ohioan Louis Bromfield, recipient of the Pulitzer Prize for fiction in 1926. In the 1930s Bromfield purchased three adjoining farms and set out to restore them by using conservation methods to rebuild the soil and restore the pastures. Bromfield designed his thirty-two room home to blend with the surroundings of Pleasant Valley in Richland County, and in keeping with the architectural influence of the Western Reserve. Bromfield lived in the house until 1956. The farm became a State Park in 1976, and as the Ohio State Parks states, "As a park, Malabar Farm is dedicated to perpetuating Bromfield's farming philosophies, preserving the Big House and its many artifacts, and providing a place where visitors can explore life on a farm and the beauty of nature." The park is fully equipped to accommodate recreational needs for both summer and winter visitors with such activities as fishing, hiking, picnicking, camping, sledding, ice skating, and cross-country skiing.

Photography provided by Ohio Department of Natural Resources, Mike Williams, Photographer

Wyandot County Museum, Historic McConnell House, Upper Sandusky, Northwest Ohio

Built in 1853, Isaac and Leefe Fowler Beery occupied the house and raised a family of four children. Twin brothers, Brooks and Isaac Beery, owned the first drygoods store in the area. Prominent local physician Robert McConnell married Isaac's daughter, also named Leefe. Their son, Fowler Beery McConnell, donated the 11-room house to the Wyandot County Historical Society in 1961. Rich with historical sites, Wyandot County is home to the Wyandot Mission built in 1824; the Old Indian Mill and Dam built in 1820. There is the Battle Island Monument where Colonial Forces fought a losing battle against the Indians and British in 1782. The historical society states that "this very community was the seat of government for the Wyandot Indian Nation . . . . The Wyandots were the last organized band of Indians to leave Ohio [moving] to a reservation in Kansas in 1843."

Photography by Robert D. Shangle

The Peter Navarre Cabin, Toledo Botanical Garden, Toledo

One of the first settlers in Toledo, Ohio, was Peter Navarre, often referred to as "Peter the Scout." He is remembered for his service as an Indian scout during the War of 1812 between the British and the United States. Records indicate that Peter Navarre's ancestory can be traced back to the King of France *and* to English Royalty of the late 1500s. The log cabin has found a secure setting within the confines of the Toledo Botanical Garden. The Toledo Convention and Visitors Association states that the Botanical Garden is "A picturesque 57 acre setting of meadows and gardens, where fragrant herbs, roses and wildflowers thrive."

Photography by Robert D. Shangle

The Covered Bridge on Clearfork River, Mohican State Park, North-Central Ohio

It is stated that "beauty is in the eye of the beholder", but one is definitely beholden to cast an admiring gaze on the beauty expressed in the above scene. The 4,500-acre Mohican State Memorial Forest "surrounds the park and contains great plant and animal diversity. . . . The Mohican State Park area was once the hunting grounds of the Delaware Indians. . . . . John Chapman, immortalized as Johnny Appleseed, frequented the region during the 1800s, caring for his apple tree nurseries." Camping, hiking, and picnicking facilities are excellent. River fishing is an exemplary sport here in the park, and in nearby Pleasant Hill Reservoir, where the Clearfork joins the Mohican River. A rightful boast is often expressed by the residents who claim that the Loudonville-Mohican Area is the Canoe Capital of Ohio.

Photography by Shangle Photographics

General Offices of Procter and Gamble in the city of Cincinnati

Without question Procter and Gamble has played an important part in most "everybody's" life, since the business is a producer of much needed and often used items in households throughout the United States and in over one-hundred forty foreign countries. Begun in 1837, brothers-in-law, William Procter, a candlemaker, and James Gamble, a soapmaker, created a small business that is now a leader in the world of business. Soap is still an important commodity for P & G, but creative business expansion has brought Procter and Gamble to a position of world importance with diversified products. The world-headquarter's building adds dimension to the skyline of Cincinnati, the home town to Procter and Gamble.

Photography by James Blank

Cutler Hall, Ohio University, Athens Campus, Southeastern Ohio

Ohio University has been part of an evolutionary Ohio since its charter in 1804. Academic endeavors began in 1808 with three students. In 1816 the cornerstone for Cutler Hall (first named College Edifice, then Center Building) was laid, with final completion in 1819. Cutler Hall, the oldest college building in Ohio, was designated a National Historic Landmark in 1966. The University states that "The College Green is the oldest part of the campus" and Cutler Hall holds a captive position on the Green along with several other handsome structures that create an ambience so dear to student life. The University goes on to say that "Since 1946 the university's service as the major educational and cultural institution in southeastern Ohio has included regional campuses in Chillicothe, Ironton, Lancaster, St. Clairsville, and Zanesville."

Photography by Robert D. Shangle

The Ohio Village in the city of Columbus

A visit to the Ohio Village takes you back to the 1860s when things were definitely different than they are today. The Ohio Historical Society operates the facility and states that the "Ohio Village represents a typical Ohio town during the 1860s. . . . *A Trek Through Time at Ohio Village.*" And time is important while touring about, as many reconstructed buildings representing the 19th-century era create the town. Take time to visit the Schoolhouse, General Store, and Tin Shop. Actual weaving takes place at the Weaving Shop and tasty treats are available at the Village Bakery. Period furniture can be seen at Clark Furniture Company store; gear for the horse and buggy can be viewed at Knight's Harness Shop; and you can move right on over to the local Blacksmith Shop for the necessary smithy work. Many more interesting places make up the village, where the "local folk" are ready to explain activities.

Photography by James Blank

The Blockhouse and Veteran's Memorial located in South Park, Mansfield, North-Central Ohio

This replicated Blockhouse was constructed in 1906, emulating the original structure built by Captain James Cunningham in 1812. The Blockhouse furnished protection to the citizens from possible Indian attack. From 1813 to 1816 the original building served as Richland County's first courthouse. This replica was constructed of materials gathered from buildings that had been erected in 1812 and 1821, providing the present building a more genuine appearance. An obelisk monument stands nearby as a memorial to John Chapman, best known as Johnny Appleseed, a "pioneer apple nurseryman . . . from 1810 to 1830." Not far from the park is handsome Kingwood Center where quality gardens and natural settings frame the French Provincial mansion that was home to industrialist Charles Kelly King.

Photography by Robert D. Shangle

A farm scene in southwest Ohio, Highland County, north of Hillsboro

Day Lilies burst forth with natural beauty the same way the farmland of Highland County bursts forth with a plentiful yield of crops. Corn and soybeans are two major crops produced in Highland County. Rich in farmland, records indicate that the county can boast of nearly 1,400 farms in an area involving 553 square miles. Burley tobacco has been a leading product also. Besides farmland in Highland County, there is plenty of recreation sites such as Rocky Fork State Park and Paint Creek State Park, both equipped with lakes that provide good fishing and water sport activities. There are excellent camping facilities, and plenty of hiking trails in such areas as Highlands Nature Sanctuary and Miller's Nature Sanctuary plus take advantage of Pike Lake State Park.

Photography by Shangle Photographics

Ross County Courthouse, Chillicothe, South-Central Ohio

In 1800 Chillicothe was given the honor of being the first designated capital of the eastern section of the Northwest Territory, and in 1802 the State Constitutional Convention was held in the stone courthouse, built in 1801. When Ohio became a state in 1803, Chillicothe became the first state capital. The current County Courthouse was completed in 1859.

Photography by Robert D. Shangle

The Rolling Hills of Southeast Ohio north of Piedmont, Harrison County

Perfect land for grazing animals and an idyllic settling to achieve tranquility and peace of mind for the troubled soul. Above ground riches seem obvious when gazing at such fertile appearing land. However, there is much below the surface in Harrison County, one of several southeast counties in Ohio that provide the nation with much needed coal. The Ohio Department of Natural Resources lists Harrison County as the second largest producer of coal in the state in 1996. Belmont County to the south ranked first and Jefferson County just east ranked third. The DNR states that "During the first half of the 19th-century, Ohio's early coal miners, primarily of English, Scottish, and Welsh descent, cut and loaded coal entirely by hand and moved the coal to local markets by means of wagons, carts, flatboats, and canal boats....From 1800 to about 1948, most of Ohio's coal was mined underground. By the 1930s, many of Ohio's underground coal mines had become fully mechanized with the introduction of coal-loading machinery." Currently, coal mining is highly mechanized and computer driven, but even so, today's coal miner still must work his physical being for total achievement required for coal mining success.

Photography by Robert D. Shangle

German Village, Columbus, Central Ohio

The German Village might well allow itself to be described as a living Time Capsule, opening itself to those who wish to tour and investigate the available history of this unique section of Columbus. The website, germanvillage.org, best explains the creation and revitalization of the district. "Today's German Village has its roots in an 1814 addition just south of the original boundaries of Columbus, which became Ohio's Capital in 1812. A small number of Germans had been in Columbus since its founding. Many were skilled craftsmen who helped build the first Statehouse. After 1830, Germans began to arrive in Columbus in far greater numbers, fleeing wars, famine, persecution, and lack of opportunity in the Old World." As in all places, growth was voluminous; world crisis effected future development and a dwindling population ensued, following depressive years. Revitalization came about through exhaustive efforts by those who supported the German Village Society, beginning in 1960. Today the German Village is a vigorous, active section of south Columbus, reflecting the same exuberance that created the initial village. It "is 233 acres of living history—a unique 'outdoor museum' where the old meets the new in a revitalized community. More than 1,600 buildings have been renewed since 1960."
Photography by James Blank

The city of Toledo and the Maumee River, Northwest Ohio

Promenade Park provides access to easy viewing of water activities on the Maumee River, one of five Ohio rivers that flow into Lake Erie, albeit the largest. Toledo, located along Maumee Bay of Lake Erie, the fourth largest of the five Great Lakes, and at the mouth of the Maumee River, was named after Toledo, Spain. It was incorporated as a city in 1837. The steady, strong growth of Toledo has stood the test of endurance. Today it is a cosmopolitan town of museums, science centers, multiple formal gardens, historic sites, and a center of education, as the home to the University of Toledo.
Photography by James Blank

Sugartree Marina in Salt Fork State Park, Guernsey County, Southeast Ohio

A most inviting sight is spacious Sugartree Marina, both for Ohio families and their invited guests, which obviously includes the handsome Canadian Goose. The Ohio Department of Natural Resources states that "The landscape of rural Guernsey County [formed in 1810] appears as a patchwork of forested hills, open meadows and misty valleys threaded by numerous streams. At the heart of this region is Salt Fork State Park, encompassing the woodlands and fields flanking Salt Fork Reservoir. As Ohio's largest state park, Salt Fork boasts recreational facilities to suit nearly every taste. . . . Spectacular wildflowers . . . and [in the] spring, the melody of wood frogs, chorus frogs and spring peepers echo through the park." Fishing is exceptional and hunting is permitted in specific areas; swimming is easily accessible along the 2,500-foot beach front. For those who wish to linger a few days in the park, there are excellent camping facilities; more refined lodging is available as well as personal cottages. The reservoir is wide-open to power boat enthusiasts, an excellent lake for water skiing.

Photography by Robert D. Shangle

Fort Meigs, Perrysburg, south of Toledo, Northwest Ohio

Building Fort Meigs was a necessity if the United States was going to win the War of 1812 against the British and keep the Indians under control. The story goes that General William Henry Harrison, at the time well known for his success win over the Shawnee Chief Tecumseh and his brother, Prophet, at the Battle of Tippecanoe, ordered the building of Fort Meigs in February of 1813. The website, www.fortmeigs.org, best describes the fort as follows: "Built in 1813 to defend the Ohio Country against British invasion, Fort Meigs constitutes the largest wooden walled fortification in North America. Today the fort stands rebuilt on its original location within a 65 acre wooded park. The ten acre fort is enclosed by a stockade wall and contains seven blockhouses, five cannon batteries, and numerous interior eight foot high earthworks." As a living museum, historical reenactments of sieges are scheduled May through October.
Photography by Shangle Photographics

The Franklin Park Conservatory and Botanical Garden, Columbus

The evolutionary development of the Franklin Park Conservatory begins when the doors were first opened to the public in 1895. The exquisite Victorian design emulates the Glass Palace constructed for the Columbian Exposition held in Chicago in 1893. In 1974 the "original conservatory or Victoria Palm House was inducted into the National Register of Historic Places," so states the Franklin Park Conservatory. Structural renovation occurred in 1989, renewing the vigor of the grand building and adding most needed room, allowing for more participation by visitors and larger exhibits. Self-guided tours through the 12,500-foot glass structure allow excursions into created habitats that introduce a tropical rain forest and arid desert, and much more. The botanical garden encloses 28 acres of varied gardens.

Photography by Robert D. Shangle

of virtually uncut beech and maple, a remnant of the big woods that once covered three-quarters of the state. Some of these magnificent hardwoods exceed seven feet in diameter, and the first branches are as much as seventy feet above the ground. Aside from the trees, there is a dammed stream that creates a six-hundred-twenty-five-acre lake for swimming, fishing, and boating.

Plenty of history has happened in southwestern Ohio since the coming of the inquisitive pioneer settler and curious investigator. Miami University in Oxford was the home of William McGuffey, author of the *McGuffy Reader*, which brought literacy to entire generations of Americans. His home on the Miami University campus, where he taught between 1826 and 1836, has been preserved with period furnishings. Another location that allegedly resulted in a book production is the Rankin House in Ripley, the restored home of an agent in the Underground Railway. (The Underground Railway, a title used to explain the activity of a group of people, was created as a clandestine enterprise to move enslaved people to safe haven, out of the slave-owning southern states into northern states and Canada. The movement was made by means of personal efforts of sympathetic people who found ways to transport the slaves without notice of the authorities. It was most active between 1830 and 1865.) Visitors can climb the stairs, which were used by slaves who were escaping to freedom, and enjoy a spectacular view of the Ohio River from the house. It is said that this is the place where Harriet Beecher Stowe heard the story about Eliza crossing the ice, an episode that she wrote into her book, *Uncle Tom's Cabin*.

Of course, southwestern Ohio is canal country, and Miami and Erie Canal Park, located between the towns of Hamilton and Middletown, preserves recreation areas, forest tracts, and some restored sections of the canal. A hiking trail along the old towpath adjoins the Rentschler Forest Preserve, an oak, gum, maple, and hickory forest with steep limestone ravines. The canals were virtually abandoned long before the turn-of-the-century, and the disastrous flooding in 1913 seriously damaged most of the canals. Natural succession is turning them back into woodlands.

In Lawrence County north of Ironton in deep southern Ohio is Dean State Park, a 2,745-acre section adjacent to huge Wayne National Forest. The State Park was established in 1916 as the second forest acquired for timber management and wildlife protection. The forest lands on this property were cutover for charcoal that was used to fire the iron furnaces that operated in Ohio before 1830, and used until richer sources of iron deposits were discovered in Michigan and Minnesota. Wayne National Forest was established in the mid-1930s following the nation's Great Depression. Farmers caught in a situation that left them unable to meet the demands of land ownership walked away from their farms and financial obligations. The Federal Government stepped in to the fray and purchased the land and then placed it within the confines of the National Forest. This land is typical Allegheny plateau limestone and coal, with which the area is underlain.

The Vinton Furnace Experimental Forest outside of Dundas occupies 1,200 acres of land that was clear-cut well over one-hundred-years ago for the purpose of making charcoal for the Ohio blast furnaces. The land now has well-aged timber, and the Mead Corporation, founded in the Chillicothe area, in cooperation with the U.S. Forest Service, has conducted research on soil types and species selection for reforestation in the varied topography of southern Ohio.

Riches
of the West

The western region of Ohio was one of the last areas to settle and develop during the rush for land in Ohio. However, the area filled up rapidly after a few minor problems were solved and when the attributes of the area became known.

While settlers were drifting down the Ohio River on flatboats in the 1780s, the area at the tip of Lake Erie was occupied by Native Americans who were becoming resentful of the encroaching settler's incursions. Toledo, located at the mouth of the Maumee River, enjoyed some settlement after General Anthony Wayne won the Battle of Fallen Timbers in 1794, but the little lakeside settlement was abandoned during the War of 1812.

The glacier smoothed lands south and west of Toledo, heavily forested and poorly drained, proved fertile and productive when cleared. The area got the boost it needed when the Wabash and Erie Canal was brought into the territory from Lafayette, Indiana, through to Toledo and was opened in 1843. Two years later, the Miami and Erie Canal was cut through some of Ohio's highest-elevation country to join the Wabash and Erie Canal at Defiance. The rolling plain country of northwestern Ohio came into its own.

Early maps of Ohio identified this area simply as "Black Swamp," a region about the size of Connecticut, stretching from Toledo south to Findlay and west nearly to Bryan. The entire area was dense forest of the type that does not mind getting its feet wet: elm, ash, cottonwood, huge oak, maple, and sycamore trees, punctuating miles of bog and swampland. Foliage was so dense that daylight could barely penetrate the lofty coverage. The area was infested with bugs such as mosquitoes, horseflies, and gnats; and creepy water rats, wolves and wildcats plus slithering snakes. Few settlers ventured into the area before the mid-19th century. Canal building in the Maumee Valley drained some of the swampland. Many of the first settlers in the area were the middle Europeans who had been brought in for canal labor. When work ended on the Miami and Erie Canal, they kept right on moving into the swamp, opening the rich black earth to sunlight for the first time. Today, all that remains of Black Swamp is the name. But just west of the city of Defiance is AuGlaize Village where a living museum maintains a replica of a typical Black Swamp farm, operated in the 19th-century style, along with an historical village.

The original Black Swamp was a relic of one of the prehistoric predecessors of Lake Erie. South and west of Toledo is another interesting place that was the sandy shore of a prehistoric glacial lake. The area is called Oak Openings, a throw back to the time when natural clearings were so rare that it made more sense to name the clearing than the forest around it. Though the shores of Lake Erie are far away, Ohio's only living sand dunes are right here at Oak Openings on this ancient beach ridge, nourishing a variety of oak species and incredible numbers of plant and animal life found nowhere else in the region. This strip of sandy soil, about twenty-two-miles long by six-miles-wide, runs a southwest drift from Sylvania on the north (west of Toledo) with an eastern boundary at Holland and Whitehouse, to the southern edge near Colton and Liberty Center, and a western boundary to Swanton. Many people believe the Oak Openings rivals in importance to that of the Barrier Islands off the state of Virginia, in as much as the Openings maintains an ecosystem of total uniqueness and great importance to the understanding of geology of the world. Known as the Oak Openings Working Group, this body of like-mined people have a mission "to encourage cooperation, communication and education among the local community, public agencies and private organizations in order to create a better understanding and appreciation for the importance of conservation of the Oak Openings. Through this partnership the group will strive to ensure the long term viability of this natural area in a manner that is compatible with the sustainable human needs of the region."

A great deal of what is worth seeing in the northern part of this region has to do with the canal construction in the 1800s. In 1932 the Toledo Metropolitan Park District signed an agreement with the state of Ohio to operate the abandoned Miami and Erie Canal lands of Lucas County as a park. Several hundred acres are set aside along the Maumee River, connecting Providence, Bend View, and Farnsworth parks. Some of the nicest views of the peaceful Maumee River are to be found here, and at Side Cut Park you can see the original limestone locks through which canal boats first entered the Maumee River in 1843. At Providence Park a picturesque dam on the Maumee, built to feed water into the canal, is the main attraction. The park, itself, is located in what was the old town of Providence, a thriving town until an epidemic of cholera closed it down. Canals got the agricultural economy of the country booming, but in less than a generation, the output of the rich farmlands became too great for canals and towboats, and railroads captured the imagination of the public. The canals declined steadily and many segments were destroyed by the heavy flooding of 1913.

The biggest boom in the northwest, literally, was in Hancock County, on the southern edge of the Black Swamp, when the Karg gas well exploded. Long before the commercial discovery of oil, itinerant preachers were warning Hancock County farmers that the fires of hell were burning directly below them. Farmers frequently had to deal with the nuisance of striking natural gas rather than water when they sank a well. A few of the farmers actually piped the stuff into their homes for heat and light.

It wasn't until the middle of the 1880s that any serious efforts were made to utilize the natural gas. In 1886 after twenty-four days of drilling, the Karg Well exploded with a *boom* that was heard across the countryside and a plume of fire shot up about one-hundred feet into the air. Before the well activity was under control, the glare of the fire was visible for some forty miles, and for a half-mile distance around it, grass grew green within a circle of snow and crickets chirped all night long. Findlay's gas supply ran low by 1890, but few people minded that problem since oil had been discovered as well as natural gas. Oil companies made their presence in the late 1880s, and the name Rockefeller became synonymous with oil business acquisitions. Findlay became the home to The Ohio Oil Company in 1905. The business name was changed to Marathon Oil Company in 1962 and it wasn't until 1990 that it changed its home address from Findlay, Ohio, to Houston, Texas.

South of Findlay near the center of Logan County is an interesting place titled Zane Shawnee Caverns and Southwind Park, just outside the town of Bellefontaine. This purchased acreage is owned by the Shawnee Nation, United Remnant Band, the first Tribally-Owned Shawnee land in Ohio since 1839, and the only Native American tribe recognized by the state of Ohio. The caverns are created on three separate levels, descending to a level of 132 feet below ground level. The Caverns invite you to explore "along the path of curved stone steps, beneath natural stone cathedrals," and to visit the Shawnee and Woodland Native American Museum.

Just a short distance from the low point in the cavern is the highest point in Ohio, Campbell Hill, at an elevation of 1,549 feet above sea level. Alpine skiing and snowboard adventure is limited to areas where higher slopes are available. It is a short distance to Zanesfield and the slopes of Mad River Mountain, which in its own right has a height of 1,460 feet.

Farther south is the city of Dayton, which deserves mention here because of the Miami Conservancy District, one of the nation's pioneering flood-control projects. Though Indians had warned earlier settlers about flooding, the attractiveness of the Miami River's direct trade route to Cincinnati overruled other considerations. The city of Dayton grew at the intersection of three rivers and a creek: the Stillwater River that flows in from the northwest; the Mad River joins from the east; the Wolf Creek arriving from the west, all entering the Great Miami River that courses through Dayton. There were floods in 1805 and 1814, but the citizens built levees and crossed their fingers. A flood control project was actually planned, contracts were let, and construction equipment was in place when the skies darkened on March 23, 1913, and rain commenced to fall. By the time the rains stopped, three days later, Dayton was drowned.

Even while the town was still mopping up from the deluge, money was subscribed for a flood control program and the state legislature passed the Conservancy Act of Ohio. The result, completed in 1922, involved five earth dams, sixty miles of levees, channel improvements, 35,000 acres of basin property, and two-hundred floodgates. The task was immense but the city of Dayton has been relatively dry ever since. The $40-million cost paid by Miami Valley property owners and public agencies in nine counties has received direct monetary benefits well surpassing the initial construction cost. The River Corridor Program finished the work of making the long-feared river a public amenity. Today, Dayton is a growing city on the western edge of Ohio, having rejuvenated itself over the years into a leader in the state. Historic significance is preserved in the Oregon Historic District that was placed on the National Register of Historic Places in 1974. The Historic community of St. Anne's Hill was also designated a Historic District in 1974 and the "progressive inner-city neighborhood, McPherson Town" is part of the rebounding downtown area of the city of Dayton, sighting itself to be "on the river's edge since 1845."

Beautiful Ohio

Original lyrics by Ballard MacDonald
New lyrics by Wilbert B. McBride
Original Music Composed by Mary Earl

I sailed away;
Wandered afar;
Crossed the mighty restless sea;
Looked for where I ought to be.
Cities so grand, mountains above,
Led to this land I love.

Chorus:

Beautiful Ohio,
Where the golden grain
Dwarf the lovely flowers in the summer sun.
Cities rising high, silhouette the sky.
Freedom is supreme in this majestic land;
Mighty factories seem to hum in tune, so grand.
Beautiful Ohio,
Thy wonders are in view,
Land where my dreams all come true.

Original Chorus:

Drifting with the current down a moonlit stream
While above the Heavens in their glory gleam
And the stars on high twinkle in the sky
Seeming in a paradise of love divine
Dreaming of a pair of eyes that looked in mine
Beautiful Ohio, in dreams again I see
Visions of what used to be.

North by Northeast

The region between Columbus and Cleveland contains some of Ohio's prime farmland and some interesting scenery and people. The territory has never become particularly industrialized, and it is full of charming towns, wineries, orchards, and other agricultural enterprises.

Drive slowly through Holmes, Wayne, and Tuscarawas counties, for this is Amish country. Yellow caution signs are posted on state and county roads that display a silhouette of a horse-drawn buggy, alerting the automobile driver to the probability of an Amish buggy. The rolling hills and well trimmed farms conspire to slow down a sight-seeing automobile driver who can then better enjoy the pastoral view and lessen a chance of an unpleasant meeting with a horse and buggy. As a religious group, the Amish live by an age-old code that has provided well for the people and still brings pride to their community.

Ashland, county seat of Ashland County, was home base for the legendary Johnny Appleseed. His real name was John Chapman and he owned an orchard over toward Mansfield. Tradition has it that he traveled these parts of Ohio planting apple orchards wherever he could, in the early days of the state's settlement. While traveling through this region, "Appleseed" warned settlers of an imminent Indian attack. "Johnny" is remembered by a handsome stone monument in South Park in Mansfield, located next to the historical Blockhouse that was so important for the protection of the citizens during the War of 1812 during British and Indian attacks.

Outside the little town of Lucas southeast of Mansfield in Richland County is Malabar Farm, a monument to the beginnings of the conservation movement in Ohio in the 1930s. Malabar, an Asian word meaning *beautiful valley*, was the home of native Ohioan Louis Bromfield. As a recipient of the Pulitzer Prize for fiction in 1926, the twenty-nine-year-old Bromfield's third novel *Early Autumn* brought much fame his way. With fame and fortune Bromfield brought his family to what he loved best, a farm in Ohio. In the 1930s he bought three adjoining farms that were in a depleted condition and in need of repair. He set out to restore them by using all the tools of the conservationist, protecting the woodland, rebuilding the soil, restoring pastures, and writing four books about Malabar. Governors, conservationists, editors, and other public figures were guests on his farm. Malabar was certainly instrumental in getting the conservation movement the recognition it needed. At Bromfield's death the farm was heavily in debt, but since 1972 Malabar Farm has been the property of the state of Ohio and became a State Park in 1976. The thirty-two room farmhouse is available for tours and the farmland has many hiking trails that allow self guided exploring trips. Camping facilities are available plus picnic areas and fishing sites. Winter activities include cross-country skiing, ice skating, and sledding. A naturalist guide is available to offer programs of natural history, forest management, and wildlife instruction. Malabar is a working farm and a symbol of the conservation movement that has done so much for Ohio and the nation.

A short distance east is Loudenville, abundantly supplied with rivers, creeks, and a lake within a short drive from the town. Loudenville considers itself the Canoe Capital of Ohio. Canoes are for rent at a number of places, and an abundant supply of unspoiled country can be seen from the smooth waterways. Between Loudenville and Wooster are some of the largest remaining inland marshes in the state, especially along Kilbuck Creek. The impoundments of the glaciers, coupled with the area's very slight slope, have been responsible for continual seasonal flooding and permanent wet area that make excellent nesting grounds for waterfowl. The Division of Wildlife manages Kilbuck Creek as a State Wildlife Area, and there is good access via the abandoned B&O Railroad grade that parallels the creek. Rabbits, quail, and forest game species can also be seen, occasionally. Dairy farming has been the traditional activity in this part of Ohio, where the land is not too wet for cultivation.

Southwest of Loudenville is Mohican State Park, surrounded by Mohican State Memorial Forest, comprised of over 4,500 acres that house stands of native hardwood trees, varying within the park location, along with stands of hemlock and white pine. The park teems with a variety of wildlife, some quite interesting such as raccoon, deer, red fox, and some not so interesting such as black rat snake and the poisonous copperhead. Fishing, hunting, hiking, and camping gather family fun activities into one location. The popular Mohican River runs through the park and is known as one of the finest canoeing rivers in Ohio. Canoeing can be an organized experience or a personal and individual experience, easily enjoyed in these fine waters. Within the park is the Lyons Falls hiking trail and a marked nature trail on the north side of Clear Fork, which is unusually informative. Winter activities present themselves in the way of snow sledding and cross-country skiing. Several ski resorts are available in this area. Near the city of Peninsula in Summit County north of Akron are ski resorts. Ski resorts in all of the areas have special celebration events at times of optimum ski conditions.

The traveler who is meandering north and east of Wooster finds himself suddenly approaching the state's most populous areas: Cleveland, Akron, Canton, and Youngstown, which forms a protective ring around the still rural Western Reserve region in the state's northeast corner.

This book has not chosen cities as a major focus, but it is interesting to think about a portion of this area at a time when the people were at the mercy of the wildlife, rather than the other way around. In 1818 just before Christmas the men of Medina County organized a hunt in Hinckley Township. Farmers had lost cattle and sheep to marauding wolves and bears; hens were lost to foxes; and deer, raccoon, and squirrels made fast work of cornfields. On December 24, 1818, in the hour just before daylight, six-hundred settlers took their places on the four sides of Hinckley Township, forming a loose battle line that closed as they drew toward the center, making lots of noise and driving the game ahead of them. By good fortune only one hunter was grazed with buckshot, and the only casualties were among the animals: countless squirrels, rabbits, foxes and raccoon, seventeen wolves, twenty-one bear, and more than three-hundred deer. One account says that the men built a fire and feasted, washing down the hot meal with cold whiskey. Many Medina County homes had fresh venison for Christmas dinner.

Those days are long gone, but the northeastern corner of Ohio has taken care to preserve some strikingly beautiful areas because of their recreational or scenic importance. Portage Lakes State Park, just south of Akron, consists of two lakes created as the summit reservoirs for the Ohio and Erie Canal. The wasting glacier left behind a large outwash belt that, today, consists of gently rolling hills covered with forests of beech and maple trees.

One of the Akron Metropolitan Parks, below the city of Cuyahoga Falls, has preserved a narrow, constricted gorge through which the river descends some two-hundred feet in about a two-mile stretch, over many waterfalls and rapids. The gorge was cut when the normal river channel to the south was blocked by glacial fill. The waterfall, for which the city of Cuyahoga Falls was named, is now buried beneath water, caused by the backwater of the Ohio Edison Company Dam.

Farther east at Fredericktown, glaciers had an even greater effect on stream flow: Little Beaver Creek and the North Fork of Little Beaver were blocked by glacial fill and forced to flow the other way by torrential melt waters. Once north flowing rivers, they later cut deep gorges for their southward flow to the Ohio River. The upland plains are covered with large oaks and white pines, while the cool, moist ravines are home to hemlocks and plants from the pre-glacial period.

Nelson-Kennedy Ledges, a state park between Cleveland and Youngstown, is another area that shows the heavily erosive effects of glacial meltwater in the form of scenic ledges and bluffs above the wooded river bottom.

Once through the "urban belt," a bit of New England is visible in the northeastern section of the state, an area that interestingly enough is known as the Western Reserve. The land was reserved for settlement by the state of Connecticut, back when Ohio *was* the west, and the name stayed with the area. In the Bath Township north of Akron and east of the village of Bath is a place where the past is officially preserved, at Hale Farm and Village. A rich history of area life, as found in the early 1800s, is revealed in the homeland property of Jonathan Hale and his wife, who developed a home and farm on land he purchased in 1810. Some original buildings, many moved from outlying sites, have been used to create the Western Reserve town of Wheatland, located nearby the farm, where period-dressed occupants greet you with open enjoyment. Discussions with "current town occupants" are presented in the "now time" of the 1848 Wheatland Township. It is truly a step back in time, and a most enjoyable experience. It is easy to observe the influence made by the early New England settlers in the neat, small towns along the back roads of the less populated counties.

Moving north toward the shore of Lake Erie is Ashtabula County; there is a special treat in store for those who enjoy covered bridges. There are sixteen covered bridges throughout the county, tucked away on quiet back roads, mostly used by Amish farmers and an occasional carload of tourists. Ashtabula County and its business folks have a big party annually, the second full week in October when the Ashtabula County Covered Bridge Festival is held, highlighted by an extensive tour of the bridges. The tour is always available, year 'round. The Harpersfield Bridge is Ohio's longest covered bridge at 228 feet. The bridge was originally built in 1868, and it was rebuilt in 1992 with a covered walkway. Locate the rivers in the county and you can find the bridges, or check with the Festival headquarters.

The Lake Erie waterfront has long been valued, both for commerce and recreation. The explorer, today, will find that Lake Erie is a well developed natural resource. The ports of Ashtabula and Conneaut are among the largest iron ore receiving centers in the world. Lake Freighters unload iron ore here for the mills of Pennsylvania and the Ohio River. But a short distance away, Geneva-on-the-Lake, which offers a variety of commercial amusements as well as camping, has been a popular resort for about one-hundred years.

Fairport Harbor and adjoining Painesville offer historic exhibits and more of the atmosphere associated with that of New England. The lighthouse at Fairport Harbor is one of the oldest in Ohio, and there is a fine view of the lakeshore from the top. Closer to Cleveland is the mile-long beach at Headlands Beach State Park, a popular spot with swimmers from the city on summer weekends.

West of Cleveland is the historic area known as Firelands. Land in this area was granted after the Revolutionary War to compensate people whose homes had been burned by the British—hence the name. It is another place where the New England style prevails in older areas. The suburbs of Cleveland stretch westward for about thirty miles along the lake. Around Vermilion the territory once again becomes a resort and is recreation oriented. Sandusky, once known as the world's largest fresh water fishing center, is a busy harbor town and has been playing host to summer guests since the end of the Civil War. There is plenty of access to scenic and recreational areas along the lake, and within miles on either side of Sandusky are facilities for camping in about a dozen or so state parks. From Sandusky it is not far to the Marblehead Peninsula, one of the most picturesque areas in Ohio. The peninsula contains hundreds of acres of orchards and vineyards residing along side the surf-pounded shores of Lake Erie. Marblehead has been one of the roughest places on the lake since the beginning of navigation in these parts, with occasional *Northeasters* that blow off the lake at hurricane velocity. The Marblehead Lighthouse, erected in 1921 and still in operation, is the oldest on the Great Lakes. The north side of the peninsula is a resort area, and Catawba Peninsula, jutting from the north side of Marblehead, is where you catch the ferryboat for the Lake Erie Islands.

The islands that are scattered throughout Lake Erie have long been popular vacation/resort areas for the people of Ohio. South Bass, with its town of Put-in-Bay, is perhaps the best known of the Erie Islands. Once the site of the luxurious Victory Hotel, a playground for presidents and millionaires, the island has slipped into a pleasant lethargy since the hotel burned in 1919. There is now a state campground where the old Victory Hotel once stood. On the east end of the island is a monument to Commodore Oliver Hazard Perry, commemorating the victory in the Battle of Lake Erie. Considered by many to be the turning point towards victory of the War of 1812, Commodore Perry "defeated and captured a British squadron of warships" opening the way for "General William Henry Harrison to conduct a successful invasion of Western Upper Canada," as stated by the National Park Service. The monument was completed in 1915 and it became a National Monument on June 2, 1936, known as Perry's Victory and International Peace Memorial.

Kelleys Island, the largest of the Lake Erie Islands, is a scant two miles from shore. An enormous granite slab, Inscription Rock, was carved with graffiti by the Erie Indians who lived there about three-hundred-fifty years ago. One of the most unusual exhibits of the glacial age will be seen here in the Glacial rooves, scorings of glacier-carried stones in the native rock of the island.

Kelleys and Middle Bass islands are the biggest of the islands and the most frequently visited of the twenty or so that make up the chain. The other islands, either privately owned or without dock facilities, are inaccessible to the general public, although boaters may enjoy the waters around them.

Important Facts

State Capital: Columbus, Ohio
                      The first capital was located in Chillicothe

State Insect: Ladybug
                      Adopted in 1975, officially naming the bug the
                      Ladybird Beetle

State Name: Ohio
                      From Native American Iriquois word meaning
                      "Great River or Good River."

State Rock Song: *Hang on Sloopy*
                      Adopted in 1985

State Song:

                      Beautiful Ohio
                      Adopted in 1989

The Buckeye Region

Glaciers did not make it as far as the Appalachian foothills in the southeastern portion of Ohio, and as a result, some of the greatest variety of terrain occurs there. This rough, hilly country, broken everywhere by river gorges, contains most of the forests and a lavish variety of Ohio's native wildlife. Ironically, this is also the area that suffered most in the past from disastrous strip mining, over grazing, erosion, and flooding. It is the home of the Muskingum Conservancy District, another pioneering effort to maintain the environment.

A considerable amount of history has occurred in this area. The Buckeye region received the first settlers who drifted down the Ohio River. The first cross-state canal cut through this country, from Portsmouth to Cleveland, and remnants of it are preserved to this date. The late 1880s saw drastic disputes in the coal mines of the Hocking Valley: during riots one summer, oil-filled coal cars were set ablaze and pushed into the mine shafts, setting underground fires that burn to this day, occasionally leaking smoke from hillsides and valleys.

Ohio's first settlement, known as Schoenbrunn—established in 1792 by David Zeisberger as a Moravian mission—is in the Buckeye region.

Today, Schoenbrunn Village State Memorial is a living museum honoring the historical period. The Buckeye Region also claims the oldest permanent settlement in Ohio, the river town of Marietta, established on the Ohio River in 1788.

Amesville, the first settlement in Athens County, was and is the site of the famous Coonskin Library. All during the winter of 1804 and 1805, the men of Amesville ran a trapline, and in the spring they loaded a wagon with bearskins, raccoon skins, wolf hides, and the like, and took them six-hundred miles to Boston. They traded the skins for $73.50 worth of books, which comprised the entire stock of one of Ohio's earliest lending libraries. The bears, raccoons, and wolves are now scarce if not gone from Ohio, but the books still exist.

The Ohio River, an influence for every area it touches, is far different here, compared to its languid appearance in the more pastoral regions west of Portsmouth. The river bustles with traffic, and the shoreline is developed to receive the cargoes of dozens of industries. This is coal mining country, and scores of manufacturing operations are headquartered on the eastern portion of the river. At this point the Ohio River is strictly business, though Marietta, in particular, has some interesting museums and historic exhibitions dealing with the river. The lover of nature and scenery will do better to move inland from the river a bit, where fruit orchards, lush pasture lands, towering forests, and various sized lakes produce an ambience far different from the purposeful hum of commerce on the river. And once inland, the Muskingum Conservancy District becomes a fact to be dealt with.

In 1938 fourteen flood-control dams were dedicated in a single ceremony, getting the Muskingum Conservancy District off to a fairly auspicious start. The District, which includes about one-fifth of Ohio's area, fans out northward and westward from Marietta as far north as Canton and Akron, and as far west as Mt. Vernon, a diverse region containing farms, mines, and cities. But, as one commentator pointed out, it all runs downhill. With every flood a great deal of the overworked land washed away to the

Gulf of Mexico. Much of the thin hillside land of this region should never have been cleared or plowed in the first place. The remedy to the problem has been the reforestation and woodland-maintenance of the region. Fourteen retaining basins form permanent lakes with several hundred miles of shoreline for recreational use and wildlife management. Many small recreation areas are located at locks and dams along the Muskingum River.

Tappan Lake, east of Uhricksville and Dennison, is formed by one of the original dams, providing flood and drought control as well as a recreational area. The lake contains the waters of the meandering Stillwater Creek, a tributary of the Tuscarawas River. The dam, fifty-two feet high and 1,550 feet long, controls drainage of about seventy-square miles. The shores are heavily wooded, and blue herons live where the water is shallow.

One of the most spectacular scenic areas in all of Ohio is the Hocking Valley, where the shifting shores of an ancient sea laid down layers of sandstone that have eroded into the deep gorges of Hocking Hills State Park. The once cultivated hilltops, now returning to forestland through natural succession, do little to prepare you for the deep canyons and impressive waterfalls at the six separate sites within the Hocking State Forest. Perhaps the most spectacular is Ash Cave, a massive sandstone overhang from which a stream drops about ninety feet into a small pool. The cavity behind the waterfall is a natural amphitheater. The tremendous overhang has remarkable acoustical qualities. During April and May the wildflowers are magnificent, and in the winter months, the waterfall freezes into a shimmering icy curtain.

Old Man's Cave west of Logan is another attraction in the park. Riddled with tunnels and stairways, offering surprising panoramic views, this area was once the home of a hermit, for the last years of his life. At the end of the gorge, Old Man's Creek tumbles over a series of ledges and waterfalls some forty feet into a catch pool, then continues on over smaller cascades and numerous potholes created within the sandstone. The cave, itself, for which this portion of the park is named, is not actually a cave, but a huge overhang, seventy-five feet above the stream and about three-hundred feet long. It is another example of soft sandstone sandwiched between harder layers, worn away by running water.

Cedar Falls, Conkle's Hollow, Rock House, and Cantwell Cliffs are the other sites in Hocking Hills State Park. The geological history of the Black Hand sandstone is about the same, but each area offers something a little different. The rugged cliffs, profuse vegetation, and shadowy canyons are best explained by seeing-is-believing. Words are few that can explain what Mother Nature has accomplished.

To the east of Hocking County is the Cumberland Mine area, where Ohio Power Company worked a minor miracle or two in rehabilitating land that had been abused. The Ohio Power Recreation Area in Morgan and Noble counties is a good example of the way mankind can put itself on the side of nature and benefit by it. Early settlers cleared the rolling hills of much of the beech and oak forest that once covered them. But typically for this area, the soil was thin and the slopes were steep: farmland wore out and erosion was a problem. The discovery of the rich coal resource underground invited further ecological depredations, and the area was extensively strip-mined until Ohio Power Company began a forestry program to replace the coal with a renewable resource—wood. Thus the land use made a full circle, back to its original woodland state.

State Parks

Northwest Region

Catawba Island State Park
    c/o Lake Erie Islands SP
    4049 E. Moore's Dock Road
    Port Clinton, OH 43452

Crane Creek State Park
    c/o Maumee Bay SP
    1400 Park Road, #1
    Oregon, OH 43618

East Harbor State Park
    1169 N. Buck Road
    Lakeside-Marblehead, OH
    43440

Grand Lake St. Marys State Park
    834 Edgewater Drive
    St. Marys, OH 45885

Harrison Lake State Park
    Route 1, Box 240
    Fayette, OH 43521

Independence Dam State Park
    27722 State Route 424
    Defiance, OH 43512

Kelleys Island State Park
    c/o Lake Erie Islands SP
    4049 E. Moore's Dock Road
    Port Clinton, OH 43452

Lake Erie Islands State Park
    4049 E. Moore's Dock Road
    Port Clinton, OH 43452

Lake Loramie State Park
    11221 State Route 362
    Minster, OH 45865

Marblehead Lighthouse State Park
    c/o Lake Erie Islands SP
    4049 E. Moore's Dock Road
    Port Clinton, OH 43452

Mary Jane Thurston State Park
    I-466, State Route 65
    McClure, OH 43534

Maumee Bay State Park
    1400 Park Road, #1
    Oregon, OH 43618

South Bass Island State Park
c/o Lake Erie Islands SP
4049 E. Moore's Dock Road
Port Clinton, OH 43452

Van Buren State Park
PO Box 117
Van Buren, OH 45889

Northeast Region

Beaver Creek State Park
12021 Echo Dell Road
East Liverpool, OH 43920

Cleveland Lakefront State Park
8701 Lakeshore Blvd. NE
Cleveland, OH 44180

Findley State Park
25381 State Route 58
Wellington, OH 44090

Geneva State Park
PO Box 429, Padanarum Road
Geneva, OH 44041

Guilford Lake State Park
5835 E. Lake Road
Lisbon, OH 44432

Headlands Beach State Park
c/o Cleveland Lakefront SP

8701 Lakeshore Blvd. NE
Cleveland, OH 44180

Jefferson Lake State Park
501 Township Road 261 A
Richmond, OH 43944

Lake Milton State Park
16801 Mahoning Avenue
Lake Milton, OH 44429

Malabar Farm State Park
4050 Bromfield Road
Lucas, OH 44843

Mohican State Park
3116 State Route 3
Loudonville, OH 44842

Mosquito Lake State Park
1439 State Route 305
Cortland, OH 44410

Nelson Kennedy Ledges State Park
c/o Punderson SP
PO Box 338
Newberry, OH 44065

Portage Lakes State Park
5031 Manchester Road
Akron, OH 44319

Punderson State Park
PO Box 338
Newbury, OH 44065

Pymatuning State Park
PO Box 1000
Andover, OH 44003

Quail Hollow State Park
13340 Congress Lake Avenue
Hartville, OH 44632

Tinker's Creek State Park
c/o West Branch SP
5708 Esworthy Road, Rte 5
Ravenna, OH 44266

West Branch State Park
5708 Esworthy Road, Rte 5
Ravenna, OH 44266

Central Region

Alum Creek State Park
3615 S. Old State Road
Delaware, OH 43015

A. W. Marion State Park
c/o Deer Creek SP
20635 Waterloo Road
Mt. Sterling, OH 43143

Buckeye Lake State Park
PO Box 488
Millersport, OH 43046

Deer Creek State Park
20635 Waterloo Road
Mt. Sterling, OH 43143

Delaware State Park
5202 U.S. 23 North
Delaware, OH 43015

Indian Lake State Park
12774 State Route 235 North
Lakeview, OH 43331

Madison Lake State Park
c/o Deer Creek SP
20635 Waterloo Road
Mt. Sterling, OH 43143

Mt. Gilead State Park
4119 State Route 95
Mt. Gilead, OH 43338

Southwest Region

Adams Lake State Park
c/o Shawnee SP
4404 State Route 125
West Portsmouth, OH 45663

Buck Creek State Park
1901 Buck Creek Lane
Springfield, OH 45502

Caesar Creek State Park
8570 E. State Route 73
Waynesville, OH 45068

Cowan Lake State Park
729 Beechwood Road
Wilmington, OH 45177

East Fork State Park
PO Box 119
Bethel, OH 45106

Hueston Woods State Park
Route 1
College Corner, OH 45003

John Bryan State Park
3790 State Route 370
Yellow Springs, OH 45387

Kiser Lake State Park
PO Box 55
Rosewood, OH 43070

Little Miami State Park
c/o Caesar Creek SP
8570 E. State Route 73
Waynesville, OH 45068

Paint Creek State Park
14265 U.S. Route 50
Bainbridge, OH 45612

Rocky Fork State Park
9800 N. Shore Drive
Hillsboro, OH 45133

Stonelick State Park
2895 Lake Drive
Pleasant Plain, OH 45162

Sycamore State Park
4675 N. Diamond Mill
Trotwood, OH 45426

Southeast Region

Barkcamp State Park
65330 Barkcamp Park Road
Belmont, OH 43718

Blue Rock State Park
7924 Cutler Lake Road
Blue Rock, OH 43720

Burr Oak State Park
10220 Burr Oak Lodge Road
Glouster, OH 45732

Dillon State Park
PO Box 126
Nashport, OH 43830

Forked Run State Park
PO Box 127
Reedsville, OH 45772

Great Seal State Park
825 Rocky Road
Chillicothe, OH 45601

Hocking Hills State Park
20160 State Route 664
Logan, OH 43138

Jackson Lake State Park
PO Box 174
Oak Hill, OH 45656

Lake Alma State Park
Route 1, Box 422
Wellston, OH 45692

Lake Hope State Park
27331 State Route 278
McArthur, OH 45651

Lake Logan State Park
30443 Lake Logan Road
Logan, OH 43138

Lake White State Park
2767 State Route 551
Waverly, OH 45690

Muskingum River State Park
PO Box 2806
Zanesville, OH 43702

Pike Lake State Park
1847 Pike Lake Road
Bainbridge, OH 45612

Salt Fork State Park
14755 Cadiz Road
Lore City, OH 43755

Scioto Trail State Park
144 Lake Road
Chillicothe, OH 45601

Shawnee State Park
4404 State Route 125
West Portsmouth, OH 45663

Strouds Run State Park
11661 State Park Road
Athens, OH 45701

Tar Hollow State Park
16396 Tar Hollow Road
Laurelville, OH 43135

Wolf Run State Park
16170 Wolf Run Road
Caldwell, OH 43724

Important Facts

State Animal:	White-tailed Deer Adopted in 1988. Largest game animal in Ohio.
State Bird:	Scarlet Cardinal Adopted in 1933.
State Beverage:	Tomato Juice Nation's leader in tomato juice production.
State Flower:	Red Carnation Adopted in 1904. Chosen as a memorial to President William McKinley.
State Fossil:	*Isoletus* Common name: Trilobite An extinct sea creature that lived some 440-million years ago in salt water that once covered Ohio. It resembled a modern-day Horseshoe Crab.
State Tree:	*Aesculus glabra* Common name: Buckeye Member of the chestnut family.

Historic Sites

Ohio Historical Center
    1982 Velma Avenue
    Columbus, OH

Ohio Village
    Interstate Hwy 71 & E 17th
    Columbus, OH

Native American Heritage

Big Bottom Park Historic Site
    State Road 266
    Stockport, Ohio

Flint Ridge Historic Site
    7901 Brownsville Road, SE
    Glenford, OH

Fort Ancient Historic Site
    6123 State Route 350
    Oregonia, OH

Fort Hill Historic Site
    13614 Fort Hill Road
    Hillsboro, OH

Inscription Rock Historic Site
    Kelleys Island
    4049 E. Moores Dock Road
    Port Clinton, OH

Leo Petroglyph Historic Site
    Off U.S. Highway 35
    Five miles north of Jackson

Logan Elm Historic Site
    State Road 361
    One mile east of U.S. 23
    South of Circleville

Miamisburg Mound Historic Site
    101 N. First Street
    Miamisburg, OH

Newark Earthworks Historic Site
    Newark Earthworks
    State Road 79
    Newark, OH
    Octagon Earthworks
    99 Cooper Avenue
    Newark, OH
    Wright Earthwork
    James & Waldo Streets
    Newark, OH

Seip Mounds Historic Site
U.S. Highway 50
Three miles east of Bainbridge

Serpent Mound Historic Site
3850 State Route 73
Peebles, OH

Shrum Mound
McKinley Avenue, One-half
mile south of Trabue Avenue
Colulmbus, OH

Story Mound
Delano Avenue, South of Allen
Chillicothe,Ohio

Settlement and Transportation History

Campus Martius Museum
601 Second Street
Marietta, OH

Lockington Locks Historic Site
Between Interstate Hwy 75 &
State Road 66
Lockington, OH

National Road/Zane Grey Museum
8850 E. Pike
Norwich, OH

Ohio River Museum
601 Second Street
Marietta, OH

Military History

Buffington Island Historic Site
State Road 124
Twenty miles east of Pomeroy

Custer Monument Historic Site
46320 Cadiz-Junction Road
Hopedale, OH

Fallen Timbers State Memorial
U.S. Highway 24 between
Maumee & Waterville, OH

Fort Amanda Historic Site
2355 Ada Road
Lima, OH

Fort Jefferson Historic Site
County Road 24
Four miles south of Greenville

Fort Laurens Historic Site
Route 1, Box 442
Bolivar, OH

Fort Meigs Historic Site
29100 W. River Road
Perrysburg, OH

Fort Recovery Historic Site
One Fort Site Street
Fort Recovery, OH

McCook House Historic Site
McCook Monument State Mem.
Public Square
Carrollton, OH

African-American Heritage

Dunbar House Historic Site
219 N. Dunbar Street
Dayton, OH

National Afro-American Museum
and Cultural Center
1350 Brush Row Road
Wilberforce, OH

John Rankin House Historic Site
6152 Rankin Road
Ripley, OH

Stowe House Historic Site
2950 Gilbert Avenue
State Route 3, U.S. 22
Cincinnati, OH

Leadership History

Adena Historic Site
Box 831, Adena Road
Chillicothe, OH

Neil Armstrong Air & Space Museum
Interstate Hwy 75, exit 111
Wapakoneta, OH

Grant Birthplace Historic Site
U.S. Hwy 52 & State Road 232
Point Pleasant, OH

Grant Schoolhouse Historic Site
318 W. State Street
Georgetown, OH

Harding House Historic Site
380 Mt. Vernon Avenue
Marion, OH

Harding Memorial Historic Site
U.S. 50,
North Bend, OH

Harrison Tomb Historic Site
Off Cliff Road
West of U.S. Hwy 50
North Bend, OH

Hayes Presidential Center Historic Site
Speigel Grove
Hayes and Buckland Avenues
Fremont, OH

Social and Economic History

Buckeye Furnace Historic Site
123 Buckeye Park Road, T-167
Wellston, OH

Cooke House Historic Site
1415 Columbus Avenue
Sandusky, OH

Glendower Historic Site
105 S. Cincinnati Avenue
Lebanon, OH

Hanby House Historic Site
160 W. Main Street
Westerville, OH

Indian Mill Historic Site
108 E. Wyandot Avenue
Upper Sandusky, OH

Museum of Ceramics Historic Site
400 E. Fifth Street
East Liverpool, OH

Ohio Ceramic Center Historic Site
State Road 93 between
Roseville & Crooksville, OH

Our House Historic Site
484 First Street
Gallipolis, OH

Piqua Historical Area
9845 N. Hardin Road
Piqua, OH

Quaker Meeting House
State Route 150 & 646
Mt. Pleasant, OH

Schoenbrunn Village Historic Site
U.S. Highway 259
New Philadephia, OH

Shaker Historical Museum
16740 S. Park Blvd.
Shaker Heights, OH

Tallmadge Church Historic Site
Public Square
Tallmadge, OH

Youngstown Historical Center
and Industry and Labor
151 W. Wood Street
Youngstown, OH

Zoar Village Historic Site
State Road 212
Canton, OH